FAMOUS PEOPLE FAMOUS LIVES

Biographies of famous people
to support the curriculum.

Florence
Nightingale

by Emma Fischel
Illustrations by Peter Kent

ESSEX COUNTY LIBRARY

First Published in 1997
by Franklin Watts
This edition 2001

Franklin Watts
96 Leonard Street
London EC2A 4XD

Franklin Watts Australia
56 O'Riordan Street
Alexandria, Sydney
NSW 2015

ISBN 0 7496 3913 X

A CIP catalogue record for this book is
available from the British Library

Dewey Decimal Classification
Number: 610.9

10 9 8 7 6 5 4 3 2 1

Series Editor: Sarah Ridley
Designer: Kirstie Billingham
Consultant: Dr. Anne Millard

Printed in Great Britain

Florence Nightingale

"Let's take a long trip round Europe," said Mrs Nightingale to Mr Nightingale, "like other rich people do."

By the time they got home they had had two children. Each was named after the city she was born in.
Parthenope ...

Parthenope   Florence

and Florence.

Naples, ancient city of Parthenope . 1819

Florence. 1820

The Nightingales lived in a
house in Derbyshire. It was a very
big house, but not big enough for
Mrs Nightingale.

So they bought a bigger house
in Hampshire too.

Florence had lots of toys and pets to play with – and twenty-seven cousins.

Life was very different then for girls. There was no school at all for poor girls and even rich ones weren't taught much.

Florence was, though, thanks to her father.

What shall we start with today?

Greek
Latin
German
French
History
Philosophy

Latin!

Florence's mother was worried. "No one likes CLEVER girls!" she said. "Piano playing, embroidery, flower arranging – that's what Florence needs to learn!"

But Florence would grow up to do a lot more than flower arranging.

When Florence was seventeen the Nightingales went to Europe again. They visited many different places and had lots of fun.

But Florence got bored in the end. She was glad when they arrived back home.

"I've had enough of parties," she said. "I'd like to study maths now, please."

Maths for a girl!

Her parents didn't think much of that idea.

So Florence found something her parents WOULD let her do. She went visiting the poor and sick. She did her best to help them.

BINDWEED COTTAGE

Florence wanted to learn more.
"I must work in a hospital now,"
she said.

Even her father got cross this
time – but, then, hospitals were
not the same in those days.

"Nursing?" said her mother.
"The shame of it! You might as
well be a kitchen-maid!"

But one person was on her side.
He was a very important man
called Sidney Herbert.

"Nursing needs people like you,"
he said. "If you really want to
learn, then start with these!"

TEN TERRIBLE DISEASES

1000 Things Wrong with Nursing

HOSPITALS TODAY

BEING POOR MEANS BEING SICK

DRAINS AND HEALTH

Florence took the books and
studied every one of them
in secret.

The more Florence read, the more she knew she had to try and change things.

Not many people wanted to be nurses. Nurses were often dirty old women who drank too much and robbed their patients.

Many nurses couldn't read or write. They had no training and most of their patients died.

When Florence was twenty-nine, a journalist called Richard Monkton Milnes asked her to marry him.

"I cannot be a good nurse and a good wife," she said sadly. "I must refuse you."

"We shall send you abroad,"
said her mother. "That will get
this crazy notion of nursing out
of your head once and for all!"

But it didn't. In fact, it did
the opposite.

While she was away Florence
found just the place to learn,
and this time no one was there
to stop her.

At the hospital Florence got
up at five every morning and
worked late into the night.

When she came home three
months later, she found plenty of
work to do right in her own house.

As Florence nursed her sick family back to health, word was spreading about her. She was asked to run a big hospital.

Florence quickly found running a hospital meant doing everything. Then a horrible disease called cholera broke out.

Soon thousands of people were ill.
Florence moved to a big hospital
packed with cholera victims.

Her family worried about her.
Cholera was very easy to catch
and many people died from it.

But disease was not the only
danger looming. A war was
going on between Russia and
Turkey. After a year, Britain and
France joined in against Russia.

Soon bad news came back.

THE TIMES

14 October 1854

MORE DIE IN HOSPITAL THAN ON BATTLEFIELD

By William Howard Russell

Wounded soldiers were taken to a place called Scutari in Turkey but there were no nurses there to help the doctors.

"Soldiers are dying needlessly. I must DO something," said Florence.

So Florence wrote to Sidney Herbert ...

just as Sidney Herbert wrote to Florence.

Sidney Herbert asked Florence
to run the hospital at Scutari.
Soon she and thirty-eight nurses
set off for Turkey.

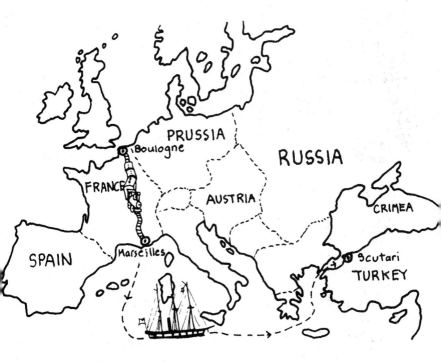

They arrived at Scutari on the
4th November, 1854. Florence
was now thirty-four years old.

The hospital was dark and filthy.
Everywhere, soldiers lay wounded
and dying. More were arriving
all the time.

Everything was dirty. There was hardly any clean water, no medicines, no bandages, no soap or towels.

Instead of getting better, most of the soldiers got worse.

"First the soldiers must be clean
and well fed," said Florence.
So she and her nurses set to work.

Then Florence rented a house.
She turned it into a laundry to
clean the sheets and clothes of
the soldiers.

She hardly even stopped to sleep.

Every day there were new problems to sort out.

What was worse, some of the doctors didn't want her there. Nor did some of the army officers.

"What does a woman know about running a hospital in wartime?" they said.

But Florence bullied and bossed and persuaded. And slowly, the hospital began to change for the better.

The wounded soldiers loved her. She did everything she could to help them get well.

She asked for books and games to be sent from England – and a chef to be sent from France.

She even wrote letters for the ones who couldn't write themselves.

And every single evening she walked through every single ward to say goodnight.

The soldiers called her the Lady with the Lamp.

Then Florence fell dangerously ill. For twelve days no one knew if she would live or die.

By now, people back in England knew all about Florence and her brave work.

Everyone waited anxiously for news.

She lives

When the war ended, big celebrations were planned to welcome her home.

But Florence didn't want a fuss, so she fooled them all.

Queen Victoria invited Florence
to stay with her in Scotland.

Florence told the Queen all about
the horrors of Scutari. "And it
will happen again if we don't
do something to change things,"
she said.

Then Florence showed the
Queen a few ideas she had had.

"We are most impressed
with her knowledge and, err,
thoroughness," said the Queen.

It wasn't just the army that Florence wanted to change.

She visited workhouses, where the poorest people lived. She went round slums, where houses were crowded together and diseases spread fast.

She tried to work out what was wrong, and then find ways to make things better.

She spent a lot of time telling important people what needed doing – even if they didn't always want to listen.

And, bit by bit, she got things done.

Sidney Herbert was worried about her. "You're doing too much," he said.

"Not enough, Sidney!" said Florence. "And now I have a few ideas about India!"

Although India was far away, it was ruled by the British then. People died in their millions from diseases or hunger.

Florence wrote letters to doctors all over India. She asked them lots of questions.

And she received lots of answers. The answers went into a report on the problems in India. It was two thousand pages long.

Florence was ill a lot between the ages of forty and sixty. But even being stuck in bed didn't stop her working – although her cats sometimes did.

A training school for nurses was set up and named after her. The students lived in the hospital while they trained.

Florence was very kind to the students. She held tea parties for them and even paid for them to go on holiday.

When Florence was eighty, her eyesight got so bad she had to stop working. That same year Queen Victoria died.

The new king, Edward VII, gave Florence a very special honour, called the Order of Merit. It was the first time it had ever been given to a woman.

Florence died when she was ninety. Everyone wanted to give her a big public funeral in Westminster Abbey.

FN
Born 1820
Died 1910

But Florence had told them not to make a fuss.

Further facts

Doctors and nurses

The first British woman who became a doctor had to go to America and Switzerland to study medicine. Only men were allowed in British universities.

The Nightingale Training School showed that there was more to nursing than changing sheets and feeding patients. For the first time nurses wore uniforms and took exams.

Sights and smells

Some of Florence's improvements
were very simple, like opening hospital
windows! Many people thought fresh
air spread diseases so the windows were
often boarded up at the start of winter.

A lot of hospitals had no lavatories,
just chamber pots under the beds.
They were filled a lot – but not
emptied half as much.

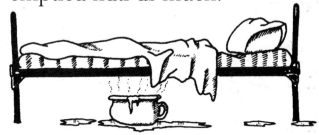

Florence brought in screens to put
round beds in her hospitals. Before
that, most operations were done in
full view of all the other patients.

Some important dates in Florence Nightingale's lifetime

1820 Florence is born on May 12, in Florence, Italy.

1837 Victoria becomes Queen of England. Florence goes on a tour of Europe.

1851 Works for three months at Kaiserwerth, in Dusseldorf, Germany.

1853 Runs her first hospital in Harley Street, London.

1854 The Crimean War begins. In November Florence goes to Scutari in Turkey, to work at the army hospital.

1855 Florence is dangerously ill but recovers.

1856 War ends. Florence returns to England and meets Queen Victoria.

1860 The Nightingale Training School for nurses opens in London.

1901 Queen Victoria dies.

1907 Florence is given the Order of Merit.

1910 Florence dies on August 13.